THERE WAS AN OLD LADY WHO SWALLOWED A PUCK

Stella Partheniou Grasso
illustrated by Scot Ritchie

Scholastic Canada Ltd.
Toronto New York London Auckland Sydney
Mexico City New Delhi Hong Kong Buenos Aires

Scholastic Canada Ltd.
604 King Street West, Toronto, Ontario M5V 1E1, Canada

Scholastic Inc.
557 Broadway, New York, NY 10012, USA

Scholastic Australia Pty Limited
PO Box 579, Gosford, NSW 2250, Australia

Scholastic New Zealand Limited
Private Bag 94407, Botany, Manukau 2163, New Zealand

Scholastic Children's Books
Euston House, 24 Eversholt Street, London NW1 1DB, UK

www.scholastic.ca

The art for this book was created using pencil and ink.
This was scanned into the computer where all the colouring was done.

Library and Archives Canada Cataloguing in Publication

Partheniou Grasso, Stella, author
There was an old lady who swallowed a puck / Stella
Partheniou Grasso ; illustrated by Scot Ritchie.

ISBN 978-1-4431-2885-8 (pbk.)

I. Ritchie, Scot, illustrator II. Title.

PS8631.A787T44 2014   jC813'.6   C2014-901824-X

6 5 4 3 2 1   Printed in Malaysia 108   14 15 16 17 18

To Arton Lankwich

— S. P. G.

*To my grandma, who loved the
races at Greenwood*

— S. R.

There was an old lady who swallowed a puck.
What rotten luck! She swallowed a puck.
And now it's stuck.

There was an old lady who swallowed a goalie,
whose padding and gear made him all roly-poly.
She swallowed the goalie to save the puck.
What rotten luck! She swallowed a puck.
And now it's stuck.

There was an old lady who swallowed a mask.
Don't even ask how she swallowed a mask.

She swallowed the mask to shield the goalie.
She swallowed the goalie to save the puck.
What rotten luck! She swallowed a puck.
And now it's stuck.

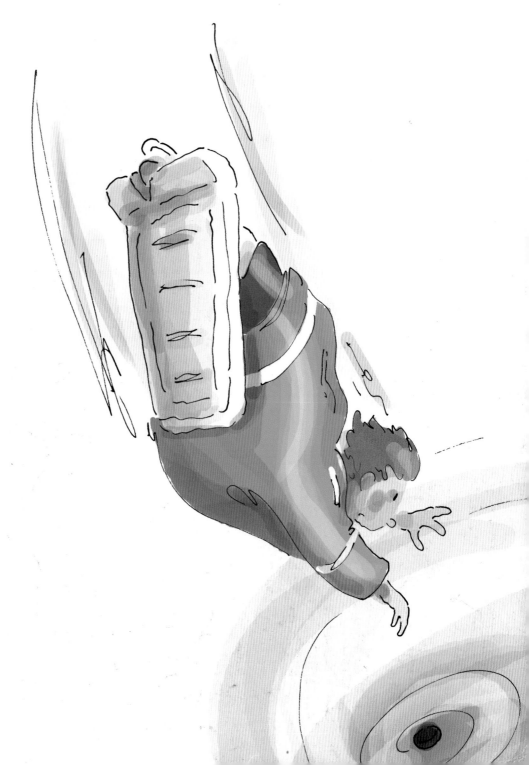

There was an old lady who swallowed two gloves.
The trapper and blocker went down with a shove.
She swallowed the gloves to grab the mask.
She swallowed the mask to shield the goalie.
She swallowed the goalie to save the puck.
What rotten luck! She swallowed a puck.
And now it's stuck.

There was an old lady who swallowed a stick.
Wow, what a trick! She swallowed a stick!

She swallowed the stick to hook the gloves.
She swallowed the gloves to grab the mask.
She swallowed the mask to shield the goalie.
She swallowed the goalie to save the puck.
What rotten luck! She swallowed a puck.
And now it's stuck.

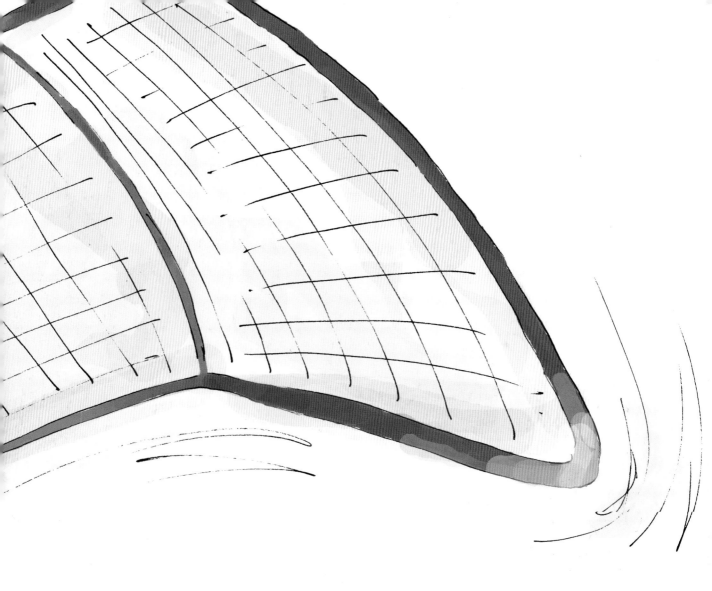

There was an old lady who swallowed a net.
How weird can she get? She swallowed a net!
She swallowed the net to catch the stick.
She swallowed the stick to hook the gloves.
She swallowed the gloves to grab the mask.
She swallowed the mask to shield the goalie.
She swallowed the goalie to save the puck.
What rotten luck! She swallowed a puck.
And now it's stuck.

There was an old lady who swallowed a rink.
What did she think when she swallowed a rink?
She swallowed the rink to hold the net.
She swallowed the net to catch the stick.
She swallowed the stick to hook the gloves.
She swallowed the gloves to grab the mask.
She swallowed the mask to shield the goalie.
She swallowed the goalie to save the puck.

What rotten luck! She swallowed a puck.
And now it's stuck.

There was an old lady who swallowed the fans.
She used both hands to shove in those fans.

She swallowed the fans to cheer at the rink.
She swallowed the rink to hold the net.
She swallowed the net to catch the stick.
She swallowed the stick to hook the gloves.
She swallowed the gloves to grab the mask.
She swallowed the mask to shield the goalie.
She swallowed the goalie to save the puck.
What rotten luck! She swallowed a puck.
And now it's stuck.

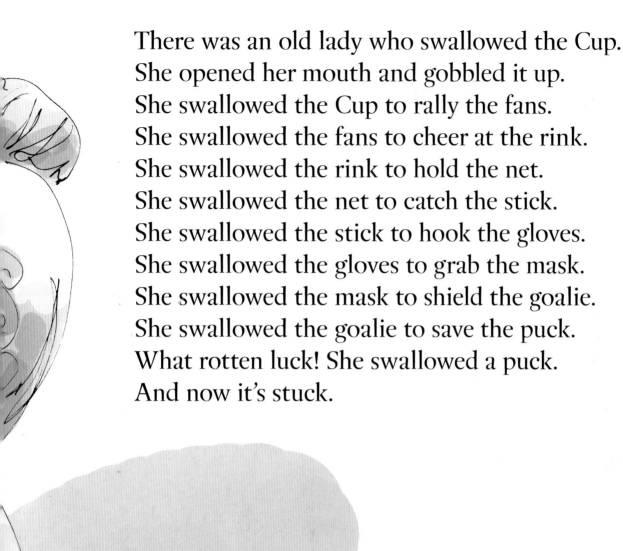

There was an old lady who swallowed the Cup.
She opened her mouth and gobbled it up.
She swallowed the Cup to rally the fans.
She swallowed the fans to cheer at the rink.
She swallowed the rink to hold the net.
She swallowed the net to catch the stick.
She swallowed the stick to hook the gloves.
She swallowed the gloves to grab the mask.
She swallowed the mask to shield the goalie.
She swallowed the goalie to save the puck.
What rotten luck! She swallowed a puck.
And now it's stuck.

Along came the ref looking surprised.
The fans were missing and the Cup they so prized.
The rink was lost, and so was the net.
It was enough to make the poor ref upset.
The stick and the gloves and the goalie's mask,
"Where have they gone?" the puzzled ref asked.
And holy moly! Where was the goalie,
whose padding and gear made him all roly-poly?

They needed the goalie to save the puck.
What rotten luck! Where was the puck?
The game was stuck.

There was an old lady who swallowed the ref and all of the players. Now there's nobody left.

She swallowed them all so they started to play,
and the old lady's belly started to sway.
The crowd went wild when the champions won.
And the old lady cheered more than anyone.

As she opened her mouth to let out a roar,
out fell the players onto the floor.
Out came the ref along with the Cup,
and the fans in the stands that she'd gobbled right up.
Out came the rink, the net and the stick.
The crowd laughed so hard at this wonderful trick.

She hollered some more,
and the gloves came unstuck.
But still no sign of that troublesome puck.
Another strong "whoop" and the mask flew out.
And the goalie rolled out with a final shout.
What wonderful luck! He caught the puck!
The crowd let out a deafening cheer,
while the old lady said, "That's the play of the year!"